What Do You See in Nature?

Gathering Da

I0805203

Leonard Clasky

COMPUTER SCIENCE For the REAL World™

Rosen Classroom™

Hiking through nature is fun. There are many plants and animals to see.

Bring a notebook to write in. You can keep track of the animals you see.

Count the number of animals as you walk. How many can you find?

You see 3 newts rest on a log. Make 3 marks under the word "newts" in your notebook.

You see 2 foxes chase one another. Make 2 marks under the word "foxes."

You see 4 fish swim down the stream. Make 4 marks under the word "fish."

You see 1 hawk flying in the sky. Make 1 mark under the word "hawks."

Look at the notebook. What do the marks tell you? Which animal did you see the most?

Which animal did you see the least? There was only 1 hawk.

How else could you gather data on your walk? You could take pictures!

Words to Know

fish

fox

hawk

newt

notebook